GALE

CENGAGE Learning

Novels for Students, Volume 33

Project Editor: Sara Constantakis Rights Acquisition and Management: Leitha Etheridge-Sims, Kelly Quin, Tracie Richardson, Mardell Glinski Schultz Composition: Evi Abou-El-Seoud Manufacturing: Drew Kalasky

Imaging: John Watkins

Product Design: Pamela A. E. Galbreath, Jennifer Wahi Content Conversion: Katrina Coach Product Manager: Meggin Condino © 2010 Gale, Cengage of the publisher.

Since this page cannot legibly accommodate all copyright notices, the acknowledgments constitute an extension of the copyright notice.

For product information and technology assistance, contact us at **Gale Customer Support, 1-800-877-4253.**

For permission to use material from this text or product, submit all requests online at **www.cengage.com/permissions.**

Further permissions questions can be emailed to **permissionrequest@cengage.com** While every effort has been made to ensure the reliability of the information presented in this publication, Gale, a part of Cengage Learning, does not guarantee the accuracy of the data contained herein. Gale accepts no payment for listing; and inclusion in the publication of any organization, agency, institution, publication, service, or individual does not imply endorsement of the editors or publisher. Errors brought to the attention of the publisher and verified to the satisfaction of the publisher will be corrected in future editions.

Gale
27500 Drake Rd.
Farmington Hills, MI, 48331-3535

ISBN-13: 978-1-4144-4171-9
ISBN-10: 1-4144-4171-1
ISSN 1094-3552

This title is also available as an e-book.
ISBN-13: 978-1-4144-4949-4

ISBN-10: 1-4144-4949-6

Contact your Gale, a part of Cengage Learning sales representative for ordering information.

Printed in the United States of America
1 2 3 4 5 6 7 14 13 12 11 10

Tangerine

Edward Bloor 1997

Introduction

Tangerine, published in 1997, is a best-selling novel for young adults by Edward Bloor. His first published work, *Tangerine* is highly regarded by both critics and readers for its strong characters, interesting setting, and compelling story. The novel was named one of the top ten best books for young adults by the American Library Association and received an Edgar Allan Poe Award nomination for best young adult novel, both in 1998.

Written in diary form, *Tangerine* takes the perspective of Paul Fisher, a legally blind seventh grader who must wear thick glasses to see. Unlike many of the adults around him and his peers, Paul is very perceptive about the problems in his family and in his new home in Tangerine County, Florida. Over the course of the novel, Paul remembers the true story of how he became blind. He also learns to tell the full truth about his family, friends, and the events he witnesses.

Tangerine uses sports to underscore aspects of the story. Paul is an enthusiastic soccer player and becomes a key member of the Tangerine Middle School soccer team. Paul's troubled brother Erik is an extremely talented placekicker for his high school football team. One recurring motif in the novel is Mr. Fisher's obsession with what Paul terms the "Erik Fisher Football Dream," as Paul and Erik's father believes that Erik can become a star in a prestigious college program, if not on a professional level.

Bloor was inspired to write *Tangerine* after he moved to Florida and began working as a public middle-school and high-school English teacher. Bloor later moved to a neighborhood—one similar to Paul's in the novel—and commuted on the back roads through citrus groves being destroyed for new housing developments. Bloor told Lynda Brill Comerford of *Publishers Weekly* that he considered *Tangerine* a *Florida Gothic*.

Author Biography

Edward William Bloor was born October 12, 1950, in Trenton, New Jersey, the son of Edward William and Mary (Cowley) Bloor. Educated in Catholic schools, he was an enthusiastic reader and began writing at an early age. As a writer, Bloor wrote copiously from seventh to twelfth grade. At the time, he was influenced by New York City's literary and theatrical scenes. During high school, he wrote plays that were produced at his school and served as the school's literary magazine editor. He was also an enthusiastic athlete, playing soccer, basketball, baseball and football. Bloor went on to play soccer and to earn an English degree from Fordham University in 1973.

After graduation, Bloor lived in New York, Boston, and England while he tried and failed to become a published author. With his family, he eventually moved to southern Florida. From 1983 to 1986, Bloor worked as an English teacher in both public middle and high schools in Fort Lauderdale. While devising educational materials for his classrooms, he became interested in publishing. Bloor left teaching and became an educational-text editor for Harcourt Brace, a publishing house, in 1986. Through his work, Bloor had to read hundreds of young adult novels and came to realize that he could write in this genre. He began writing, often by dictating into a recorder while commuting to work and while doing such tasks as mowing the lawn.

Through Harcourt, Bloor published his first young adult novel, *Tangerine*, in 1997. It eventually sold nearly a million copies. With the success of the novel, Bloor frequently traveled to book signings and speaking engagements at schools. Bloor continued to both work at Harcourt and write other young adult novels. Bloor also achieved success with his next novel, *Crusader* (1999). Like *Tangerine*, *Story Time* (2004) was nominated for an Edgar Allen Poe Award for best young adult novel. In the years that followed, Bloor wrote the popular novels *London Calling* (2005) and *Taken* (2007). Since then, he's been living, working, and writing in Florida with his schoolteacher wife, Pamela Dixon, and their children, Amanda and Spencer.

Plot Summary

At the beginning of *Tangerine*, seventh grader Paul Fisher, wearing his thick glasses, is helping his mother Caroline finish closing up the family home in Houston. They are moving to Lake Windsor Downs in Tangerine County, Florida. As he and his mother drive away from their old home, he has vague memories of telling his parents that his elder brother Erik tried to kill him, but his mother dismisses it because of Paul's poor eyesight.

Part 1

FRIDAY, AUGUST 18

As Paul and his mother arrive in Lake Windsor Downs, Paul talks about his father's obsession with Erik, a star placekicker, landing at a big-time college and perhaps someday going pro.

SATURDAY, AUGUST 19

The next morning, Paul smells fire and alerts his mother. She calls the fire department and is distressed to learn that it is a muck fire that has been burning for years and will continue to burn because it is nearly impossible to put such fires out. Paul's mother is unhappy to know that she must live with the situation.

SATURDAY, AUGUST 19, LATER

Paul rides his bike and explores his new surroundings. When he arrives home, he finds his mother talking to Mr. Costello, the head of the development's homeowners' association. Erik and his father arrive home, and Mr. Costello learns that Erik is a high school football star. He goes home to get his son Mike, who is also a highly regarded football player, and they talk about the team.

MONDAY, AUGUST 21

Paul's mother drives him to Lake Windsor Middle School. She is displeased to learn that the seventh and eighth graders, including Paul, have all their classes in portable buildings behind the main school building. She tells Mrs. Gates, the school's principal, that Paul is legally blind without his glasses. Paul thinks he can see clearly and cares only about joining the school's soccer team.

WEDNESDAY, AUGUST 23

Paul, his mother, and his father go to the high school's football tryout camp and watch Erik and the other players demonstrate their skills. After a downpour, Paul introduces himself to Joey Costello, Mike's little brother, and other kids playing with a soccer ball. Paul is not impressed by their abilities.

MONDAY, AUGUST 28

On the first day of school, Paul has a flashback to an early day of kindergarten when his brother made fun of his impaired vision at the bus stop. Erik said that Paul stared at a solar eclipse without protection and damaged his eyes. Although this story gets repeated, Paul does not completely believe it. At school, Paul demonstrates his independence by dismissing his guide for the day.

WEDNESDAY, AUGUST 30

At home, Paul listens to Erik practicing his kicking with the help of a third-string player on the team, Arthur Bauer. Arthur has an SUV and drives Erik around, because Erik does not drive. Paul ponders how Erik will give Arthur enhanced social status.

THURSDAY, AUGUST 31

Paul learns that soccer tryouts will start the next day. To prepare, he goes running with Joey. Joey points out Mr. Donnelly's house, which has been struck repeatedly by lightning. Paul offers a complicated theory about why it happened.

FRIDAY, SEPTEMBER 1

After school, Paul makes the team because no one is turned away. However, only the top fifteen players go to away games. Wearing thick prescription goggles, Paul is nicknamed Mars by teammates. He impresses his teammates with his skills and he is sure he will be the starting goalie.

TUESDAY, SEPTEMBER 5 TO THURSDAY, SEPTEMBER 7

At home, Paul learns from Erik and Arthur that Mike died that afternoon at football practice. He was struck by lightning when he leaned against a goalpost that was hit. When they are outside alone,

Erik and Arthur make fun of Mike, how he died, and how his little brother reacted to the situation. Paul is disgusted by them.

Media Adaptations

- *Tangerine* was recorded as an audio book read by Ramon de Ocampo. It was released by Recorded Books in 2001.

- Edward Bloor maintains a web site at http://www.edwardbloor.net that includes information on *Tangerine* and other novels. It also provides a biography of the author.

At school, there is little attention paid to the death. Paul realizes there are only a few good players on his team and that his brother is key to understanding what he cannot remember how he became blind. The next day, Caroline organizes a meeting at the family home about having football practice during an unsafe time of the day. Through her efforts, practices are moved to mornings.

FRIDAY, SEPTEMBER 8 TO FRIDAY, SEPTEMBER 8, LATER

Paul is upset to learn that he has been kicked off the soccer team because his mother filled out a form that identified him as handicapped. Although Paul's mother assures him that his father can work it out with the coach, Paul's only option is to become the team's manager. Caroline apologizes to Paul for filling out the form and killing his dream. Later that night, the whole family goes to Mike's viewing, where Paul offers support to Joey.

SATURDAY, SEPTEMBER 9

While riding with his mother and Joey to a carnival, Paul learns that Tangerine County used to be the "tangerine capital of the world." At the carnival, Joey points out some kids from Tangerine Middle School that he thinks they need to avoid. Paul admires their skills with a soccer ball. Joey and Paul meet up with other kids from their school, but Paul gets left behind when he gets enthralled by the "Boy Who Never Grew" exhibit in the "Wonders of the World" freak show. As Paul leaves the exhibit, he sees the kids from Tangerine Middle waiting to go inside. Paul does not see Joey again until Caroline comes to pick them up.

MONDAY, SEPTEMBER 11

On a rainy school day, Paul is called into the office with other boys who were at the carnival. They are asked if they vandalized an exhibit in the freak show, they deny it, and Paul accuses the soccer-playing kids from Tangerine Middle School. Walking back to class with the other boys, Paul worries that those kids will learn he told on them. Before they can get back to class, the portable classrooms began sinking because a sinkhole has opened under the field. Paul and Joey help save students trying to escape the portables.

MONDAY, SEPTEMBER 11, LATER TO FRIDAY, SEPTEMBER 15

While the students and city deal with the collapse of the sinkhole, Paul is proud of his actions. He is out of school for several days while his father, who works for the city as a civil engineer, is promoted to director of civil engineering for the county. It has come to light that his boss, Old Charley Burns, had been taking bribes and allowing development without inspections.

At a later meeting, Paul learns that he can either attend Lake Windsor on a split schedule or transfer to Tangerine for the remainder of the semester. Paul tells his parents that he will go to Tangerine and that there will be no paperwork filled out identifying his blindness so he can play soccer. They agree.

Part 2

MONDAY, SEPTEMBER 18

Paul's mother reluctantly drops him off at Tangerine for his first day. He is assigned an escort for the first day, Theresa Cruz, to show him around. She does not talk much to him, except when Paul asks about the soccer team. Her twin brother Tino is a good player on the team. Paul also discovers that the soccer players who vandalized the carnival are on the team. After school, the team coach, Ms. Bright, allows him on the team but only as a backup. His mother picks Paul up after practice and tells him she removed the form that put him in the handicapped program from his paperwork.

TUESDAY, SEPTEMBER 19

At lunch the next day, Paul meets the tough soccer kids—Victor, Tino, and Hernando—who had been suspended and went to "vandalism jail" for breaking the freak-show exhibit. They admit to their actions, and Paul succeeds in fitting in with them. Later, at soccer practice, Paul is impressed by their talent.

WEDNESDAY, SEPTEMBER 20

When Joey comes over to show Paul his soccer uniform and see Paul's, Erik and Arthur make fun of Mike Costello and Joey's reaction to his death. Joey wants to confront them, but Paul tells him it is not worth it.

FRIDAY, SEPTEMBER 22 TO FRIDAY, SEPTEMBER 22, LATER

Tangerine's first soccer game is an away game at a school with both nasty players and mean-spirited fans. During the first half, Paul is amazed by his team's abilities. After Tino starts punching an opposing player for upending him, his coach sends Paul in as a replacement center forward. Paul gets pulled from the game, too, for reacting when he gets mud put in his eyes. The team wins by a score of 2 to 1.

SATURDAY, SEPTEMBER 23

The whole Fisher family attends Erik's first football game. Erik looks like a fool when he kicks at air after not being informed his team would be using a trick play to win the close game. Erik is further humiliated when the local news airs the clip of his dramatic fall into the mud.

TUESDAY, SEPTEMBER 26 TO FRIDAY, SEPTEMBER 29

No one from Paul's family attends his first home soccer game. He is impressed by this school's level of talent as well as the skills of his own team. After Victor is sent to the hospital by Coach Bright for a bleeding wound on his forehead, Paul plays in the second half of the game as Victor's replacement. Paul unexpectedly scores his first goal of the season, and his team wins easily. Victor congratulates him. Later at home, Paul is befuddled when Cara Clifton calls him on the telephone and asks him if he likes Kerri Gardner. He calls his friend Joey, who tells him Kerri was probably listening in on the conversation to find out what he would say about her.

Because Paul's mom calls the local newspaper about the outstanding talent of the girls on his team, Mr. Donnelly from the newspaper shows up at their practice. Shandra runs and hides when she sees the reporter, while the coach questions his motive for covering the story. In the end, only Maya is mentioned in the paper.

MONDAY, OCTOBER 2 TO THURSDAY, OCTOBER 5

Though recent transfer student Joey is reluctant, Paul has him join a group with Henry D., Theresa, and Tino for a class project. Theresa takes charge of the group and tells them they are going to focus on a new type of tangerine her brother Luis has invented, the Golden Dawn. While working on his class project on his father's computer, Paul listens to a meeting of the homeowners' association. Paul learns about a rash of robberies of valuables in the homes that have been tented for the fumigation of insect pests.

On Thursday, Paul is invited to the Cruz house to meet Luis for the project after school and for soccer practice. At the Tomas Cruz Groves/Nursery, Luis shows them around, teaching them about his groves, his nurseries, and how he created the Golden Dawn variety of tangerine. Paul is very impressed and Luis invites him to come again. At home, Paul has another flashback about losing his vision when the family lived in Huntsville, Alabama.

THURSDAY, NOVEMBER 2 TO SATURDAY, NOVEMBER 4

Over the past busy month, Erik has become the star player on his high school team, while Paul has regularly substituted for other players on his winning middle-school soccer team. Acting on Luis's invitation, Paul has his mom drop him off at Cruz Groves on Saturday, November 4. Although Tino is hostile, Luis has Paul help lay hoses around the baby trees and then cut holes in them. After this hard day of work, Tino has new respect for Paul, and Paul tells him that he was the one who told on them that day at the carnival. Tino gives him one kick in the "backside" as punishment.

SUNDAY, NOVEMBER 5

The Fisher family spends the evening at Mr. Donnelly's house. Mr. Donnelly is a booster for the University of Florida, and knows the football coaches there. His guests also have connections to college football. The family hopes to bring Erik's skills to their attention. While Erik is the center of attention, Donnelly also talks to Paul. At home, Paul has another memory about the past and his eyes involving a visit from his grandparents.

TUESDAY, NOVEMBER 7 TO FRIDAY, NOVEMBER 10

In Paul's last home game, he starts at left wing and gets a goal. The game gets called when it starts raining and it goes into the book as a "no game." Friday is the last game of the season and one that determines the championship between Tangerine and Lake Windsor. There is a bigger crowd, which includes Paul's mother. After Victor gets punched in the face by an opposing player, Paul goes into the game in his place. The game is rough, and Shandra gets hurt. Paul replaces her as goalie and lets in one goal. At halftime, Coach Walski tells Coach Bright that Paul is ineligible to play and threatens to turn him in to the referee. Coach Bright counters with the fact that Shandra is Antoine Thomas's sister and that the star football player does not live in Lake Windsor. Walski backs off, and the game continues. The game ends in a tie, and Tangerine is the league champion.

Part 3

MONDAY, NOVEMBER 20

Paul's school-project group comes over to his house to make some decisions about their paper. While they play outside with a soccer ball, Erik and Arthur show up and Erik makes a condescending remark. Tino stands up for himself, and Erik hits him hard. The group leaves, and Paul wonders what he should have done.

TUESDAY, NOVEMBER 21

Still reeling from yesterday's events, Paul accompanies his mother on her errands. Because his mother has a meeting with Erik's school guidance counselor, Paul watches the end of football practice from under the bleachers. He witnesses Luis confronting Erik about Tino, and Arthur hitting Luis's head with a blackjack (a type of small weapon). Antoine Thomas and some other players assist Luis.

THURSDAY, NOVEMBER 23, THANKSGIVING

Writing about yesterday, Paul says that he notices that many kids have been absent from school. Henry D. tells him that it is because of the freezing weather, and that the kids are helping their families save their crops. Paul and Henry D. volunteer at the Cruz's' after school. They work hard to save as many trees as they can using various methods, although Paul is made to stay inside and rest at 2:00 AM Before Luis goes out again, Paul tells him that he witnessed Arthur using the blackjack on his head. In the morning, Paul apologizes to Tino for what happened at his house. Luis also tells him that he, Antoine, and another guy on the football team will get retribution on Erik and Arthur. When Paul's mother picks him up, he is tired and sick so she lets him stay home from Erik's last football game.

FRIDAY, NOVEMBER 24

Paul learns from his dad that the center on the football team seemed to deliberately snap the ball poorly every time Erik had a chance to kick for a point in his last game. Antoine was its star. Paul also makes his dad understand that he never showed any interest in his soccer games this season. A neighbor alerts them to smashed mailboxes in the neighborhood. When Paul goes outside to check them out, he smells the smoke of the muck fire. It triggers the trace of a memory and causes him to faint.

MONDAY, NOVEMBER 27

Paul's mother insists that he stay home from school because of illness. Paul is shocked when Erik comes home unharmed, and later when Kerri calls to ask him to go to a party at Joey's after the football awards banquet on Friday.

TUESDAY, NOVEMBER 28

Going back to school, Paul learns that Luis Cruz was found dead yesterday in one of his groves. Luis died of an aneurysm that doctors believe was caused by a blow to his head. Although others believe Luis was hit by a branch during the freeze, Paul goes home sick and investigates the possibility that the blow from Arthur killed him. Paul concludes that Arthur was at fault.

WEDNESDAY, NOVEMBER 29

Staying home again, Paul gets a call from Theresa, who tells him not to come to Luis's funeral on Thursday because something might happen to him. Paul realizes that they all knew about Luis getting hit by Arthur.

THURSDAY, NOVEMBER 30

Home again, Paul puts on his suit, goes outside by the gray wall, and—in a tribute to Luis—digs until he hits the soil of the tangerine grove.

FRIDAY, DECEMBER 1

Paul remains home during the day, but goes to his brother's football awards that night. During the ceremony, Tino and Victor show up. Tino attacks the unsuspecting Erik, while Victor attacks Arthur. The crowd at the ceremony jumps up and intervenes. Victor escapes, but Tino is put in a headlock by Coach Warner. As the coach tries to take Tino away, Paul jumps on him and Tino is able to make his escape. Paul's father is furious and demands to know who attacked Erik and Arthur, but Paul runs out as well. As he makes his way home, Paul is stopped by Erik and Arthur. Paul shows no fear through Erik and Arthur's attempts to intimidate him. Erik loses his temper before they leave.

When Erik calls Arthur "Castor," Paul remembers what happened to him when he lost his sight. He was about five when Erik and his friend, Vincent Castor, spray-painted a wall. Paul knew they had done it, although he told no one. Erik believed that Paul told on Castor, and punished Paul by holding him down while Castor spray-painted into Paul's eyes. His mother found Paul unconscious and drove him to the hospital.

When Paul arrives home and confronts his parents about what happened. His father says they did not tell him because they did not want him to hate his brother. Paul makes his father cry when he says, "So you figured it would be better if I just hated myself?"

SATURDAY, DECEMBER 2

Joey alerts Paul that Betty Bright is at Mr. Donnelly's house. Paul learns from Shandra that Antoine has decided to tell the truth about his residency because of what happened to Luis and because of the many lies he has had to tell. Antoine later encourages Paul to speak the truth as well, as he knows Paul witnessed what happened to Luis.

SUNDAY, DECEMBER 3

Mr. Donnelly's story causes a stir. Based on Antoine's sworn statement, all of Lake Windsor's victories and all school records set while he was on the team are nullified. Although the community vilifies Antoine, Paul points out to his father that the truth was right in front of everyone because Antoine was never in Lake Windsor except for school and games.

SUNDAY, DECEMBER 3, LATER

At a meeting with local residents who have been robbed, along with the Fisher and Bauer families, Erik and Arthur sport their beat-up faces. Paul's mother informs the people who had been robbed that Erik and Arthur have been committing the crimes. She found the evidence in the family's storage unit, and that she has arranged for items to be returned. The fathers of Erik and Arthur ask those present to accept the return of the items as restitution and that they not press charges. The victims agree reluctantly to the plan.

As the meeting ends, Arthur is arrested for

Luis's murder. Arthur's father tells the arresting officer that Arthur is innocent. Paul speaks up and tells the police what he saw Arthur do with the blackjack. Paul also states that Erik told Arthur to do it, and Erik admits to his role in the crime. After the law-enforcement officials leave, Paul's grandparents show up for their scheduled short visit. His grandparents remind his mother and father that they believed Erik needed help when he hurt Paul.

MONDAY, DECEMBER 4

After Paul hands Theresa the final copy of their report, he is expelled for the rest of the school year for "assaulting a teacher or other School Board employee." Paul will complete seventh grade at the local Catholic school. As he leaves Tangerine, the kids congratulate him. On the car ride to the mall, he tells his mother he will be going back to Tangerine Middle School and its soccer team next year.

TUESDAY, DECEMBER 5 TO TUESDAY, DECEMBER 5, LATER

The investigation into the murder of Luis continues, and Paul's dad washes his hands of Erik. Tino calls and makes peace with Paul. Tino also invites Paul to come and help fill the orders for the Golden Dawn tangerine whenever he wants. Later, Paul completes his statement for the police.

WEDNESDAY, DECEMBER 6

Paul has his first day at St. Anthony's. His father drives him to school, pointing out the tree planted in memory of Mike Costello along the way.

Characters

Adam

Adam is a student at Lake Windsor Middle School. He seems close to Kerri at the carnival.

Tommy Acoso

A native of the Philippines, Tommy is a student at Lake Windsor Middle School and one of the best players on its soccer team.

Ms. Alvarez

Ms. Alvarez is Paul's homeroom teacher at Lake Windsor Middle School.

Arthur Bauer Jr.

A mediocre player on the high school football team, Arthur becomes Erik's flunky. He serves as Erik's holder for kicking, drives him everywhere in his SUV, and becomes his enforcer, as when he hits Luis Cruz on the side of the head with a blackjack. Arthur is also responsible for the actual burglaries in Paul's housing development. At the end of the novel, he is arrested for his crimes.

Arthur Bauer Sr.

The father of Arthur and Paige, he works as a building contractor and a major in the Army National Guard. He tries to keep his son's future intact by getting his robbery victims to agree not to press charges in exchange for the return of the items. His tactic works in the short term, but his son is eventually arrested for his role in the death of Luis Cruz.

Paige Bauer

Paige is Arthur's sister, a sophomore at Lake Windsor Middle School and a cheerleader. Paul thinks she is dating Erik.

Brian Baylor

Brian is a senior on the Lake Windsor High School football team. He plays center and helps sabotage the last game of the season for Erik.

Bud Bridges

Bud Bridges is the principal at Lake Windsor High School. His wife is a teacher at Lake Windsor Middle School.

Mrs. Bridges

Mrs. Bridges is Paul's language-arts teacher at Lake Windsor Middle School. Her husband is the principal at Lake Windsor High School.

Betty Bright

A locally raised track-and-field star who competed internationally, Betty Bright is the soccer coach at Tangerine Middle School. She lets Paul on the team and allows him to play. Coach Bright often acts in support of her players, but does not hesitate to punish them when necessary.

Old Charley Burns

Old Charley Burns is the head of Tangerine County's Civil Engineering Department at the beginning of *Tangerine*. Because he has taken bribes and permitted unchecked, shoddy construction in the area, a sinkhole develops. It takes out the portable classrooms behind the middle school. Burns uses his illegally obtained money to attend as many stock-car races as possible. Soon after Burns's transgressions come to light, he has a heart attack and dies in his lawyer's office.

Vincent Castor

Vincent Castor was Erik's flunky when the family lived in Huntsville, Alabama. It is Vincent who actually sprayed the paint in Paul's eyes when Paul was about five years old. The act made Paul legally blind, but no consequences for Vincent are mentioned. Erik calls Arthur "Castor" late in the book because of the similar role Arthur plays in his life.

Cesar

Cesar is a reserve player on the Tangerine Middle School team.

Cara Clifton

Cara is a student at Lake Windsor Middle School. She is Joey Costello's girlfriend and a close friend of Kerri Gardner.

Mr. Jack Costello

A lawyer and head of the Homeowners' Association, Jack Costello is the father of Mike and Joey Costello. He becomes distraught when his son accidentally dies after being struck by lightning during football practice.

Joey Costello

Joey Costello is Mike Costello's younger brother and is in the same grade as Paul. Like Paul, he enjoys soccer, but Joey is not a great player and eventually quits. Joey becomes very upset when Mike dies but continues to date and attend school. Sometimes a friend of Paul, Joey also briefly attends Tangerine Middle School but responds poorly to Paul's friends there and does not fit in. So, he returns to Lake Windsor Middle School.

Mike Costello

The son of Jack Costello and the older brother of Joey Costello, Mike is a star football player at Lake Windsor High School. He is a lineman, and then becomes the number two quarterback. Football is not Mike's whole life before his death as he has already been accepted into the School of Engineering at Florida State University. In early September, Mike dies during football practice when he is struck by lightning while leaning against a goalpost.

Luis Cruz

Luis Cruz is the older brother of Tino and Theresa Cruz and the son of Tomas Cruz. He walks with a limp because of a childhood work accident with the clippers used to harvest tangerines, but he played goalie for his school soccer teams. Luis's passion is his work, especially his development of a new type of tangerine, the Golden Dawn. Luis appreciates Paul's interest in his work and allows him to help the family business several times. Luis dies of an aneurysm after Arthur hits him in the head with a blackjack on Erik's orders.

Theresa Cruz

Theresa Cruz is a student at Tangerine Middle School. She is the twin sister of Tino Cruz, the sister of Luis Cruz, and the daughter of Tomas Cruz. She is a good student and leads Paul around on his first days at Tangerine. Theresa is friendly with Paul and appreciates his completion of their class project on Luis's Golden Dawn tangerine.

Tino Cruz

Tino Cruz is a student at Tangerine Middle School and a good soccer player on his school's team. He is also the twin brother of Theresa, the brother of Luis, and the son of Tomas Cruz. Although he does not respect Paul much when he comes to Tangerine, he comes to appreciate him after Paul helps save the family's citrus trees during a freeze. Tino does not like to back down from a challenge, and he does not fear the consequences of inflicting retribution. He is suspended several times during the school year for his actions.

Tomas Cruz

Tomas Cruz is the owner of the grove and nursery where his oldest son, Luis, works. He is also the father of Tino and Theresa.

Gino Deluca

A student at Lake Windsor Middle School, he is arguably the best player on their soccer team. Gino serves as the team's captain.

Henry Dilkes

Henry Dilkes, also known as Henry D., is the younger brother of Wayne Dilkes, and he is a student at Tangerine Middle School. He plays soccer and is in the class project group with Paul, Tino, and Theresa. Henry is a good friend to the Cruz twins as well as Paul. With Paul, he works all night to ensure the family's citrus trees survive a freeze.

Wayne Dilkes

The brother of Henry D., Wayne Dilkes is a local volunteer firefighter, spray-truck driver, and exterminator who kills termites and mosquitoes in the Lake Windsor development where Paul resides. Wayne also gives Paul and his brother rides to the Cruz family's grove, sharing his knowledge about the infestations with them along the way.

Bill Donnelly

Bill Donnelly, often called Mr. Donnelly by Paul, lives in his development. His home has been hit by lightning three times, making it impossible to sell and insure it, so he has ten lightning rods along the roof. Mr. Donnelly also is the father of Terry Donnelly and works as a reporter. He writes stories on the amazing girls on Paul's soccer team, on Betty Bright, and on the truth about Antoine Thomas's residency. Mr. Donnelly is also a University of Florida booster and attempts to help Erik and Mr. Fisher by introducing them to other boosters.

Terry Donnelly

The son of Bill Donnelly, he resides with his

father in the same development as Paul's family. He plays football at Lake Windsor High School.

Sergeant Edwards

A member of the Tangerine County's Sheriff Department, Sergeant Edwards is in charge of the robbery cases involving Erik and Arthur.

Dolly Elias

Dolly Elias plays fullback and is a good player on the Tangerine Middle School soccer team.

Caroline Fisher

Caroline Fisher is the mother of Paul and Erik, and the wife of Mr. Fisher. While she is more supportive of Paul than her husband, she often so caught up in her own activities and problems that she does not always know what is going on in Paul's life. She does drive him most places, though, and takes charge of dealing with his schools and buying him clothes. Over the course of the novel, she becomes the head of the Architectural Committee of the Homeowners' Association and serves as the block captain for the Neighborhood Watch patrol. If there is a problem, Caroline makes a call or holds a meeting at her home. More than her husband, Mrs. Fisher is at least somewhat aware that Erik's football dreams might not come to fruition early on. She becomes gravely concerned when she discovers the stolen items Erik has been putting in the family storage facility and talks about the situation with the sheriff. Much to her husband's dismay, she has a close relationship with her parents, who visit toward the end of the novel. In *Tangerine*, she acts on her maternal instincts and does her best to support Paul, her husband, and even Erik.

Erik Fisher

Erik Fisher is Paul's high-school-age brother and the reason why Paul is blind. Erik has a mean—if not sadistic—streak, and an ability to manipulate those around him, including Arthur and Paul. He is prone to rages and does not always have control of himself. While Erik only shows a hypocritical side that is positive and polite to most adults, he beats up Tino, has Arthur participate to Luis's murder, and robs local houses with Arthur's help. In the end, Erik's true nature catches up to him, and he loses his football dream to the legal system. It is unclear at the end of the novel what his fate will be.

Mr. Fisher

Paul's father, Mr. Fisher, has come to Florida to work as a civil engineer for Tangerine County's Civil Engineering Department. After a sinkhole develops at the Lake Windsor Middle School and his former boss Old Charley Burns is revealed to be corrupt, Mr. Fisher becomes the director of the department. More important to the story, Paul's father is the tireless supporter of what Paul terms "the Erik Fisher Football Dream." Essentially ignoring Paul, his needs, and his soccer games, Mr. Fisher focuses on turning Erik's admitted talent for placekicking into a football scholarship at a prestigious school, if not a career in the National Football League. Every action of Mr. Fisher's focuses on that goal until the end of *Tangerine*, when he learns that his dismissal of Paul's needs, including the need to know the truth about why he is legally blind, has deeply affected his young son.

Paul Fisher

The hero, narrator, and primary character in *Tangerine*, Paul Fisher is a seventh grader who has moved to Lake Windsor with his parents and older brother, Erik. Legally blind because his brother and his brother's friend Vincent Castor sprayed paint in his eyes when Paul was only about five years old, Paul wears thick glasses that allow him to see and to play his favorite sport, soccer. As Paul struggles to remember what his brother did to him all those years ago, he encourages others, identifies with the downtrodden, and does his best to help other people, such as the Cruz family and kids at his school. He does not want to be labeled as *handicapped* as he believes he is the only one in his family, and sometimes his local environment, who can truly see. Paul wishes his parents, especially his father, were not so blinded by Erik and his needs, as Paul and his accomplishments are often ignored in favor of Erik's talents on the football field. Over the course of the novel, Paul learns to trust himself and not fear people like Erik. With his newly found confidence, Paul tells the truth about Erik and Arthur when they contribute to Luis Cruz's death. Although this truth makes his family life difficult, it strengthens Paul and helps him continue to grow at the end of the novel.

Kerri Gardner

Kerri Gardner is a student at Lake Windsor Middle School and a friend of Cara Clifton. She first meets Paul when she is assigned to guide him around on his first day, but allows him to go on his own when he asks. Paul has a crush on her and she shows interest in him, but they never get to spend time together.

Mrs. Gates

Mrs. Gates is the principal of Lake Windsor Middle School.

Grandmom and Grandpop

Paul's maternal grandparents, Grandmom and Grandpop, play a limited role in his life but call regularly and express interest in him. His mother is close to them, but his father does not particularly like them or want them around. They visit shortly after the truth about Erik and Arthur comes to light, and they remind Paul's mother and father that they believed Erik needed help when he hurt Paul years ago.

Victor Guzman

Victor Guzman is one of the star players on the Tangerine Middle School team, and its leader. Like Tino Cruz, Victor does not easily back down from a challenge, nor does he fear the consequences of inflicting retribution. He is suspended several times during the school year for his actions. Although Victor initially challenges him, he also comes to appreciate Paul's soccer skills and loyalty as a friend.

Hernando

Hernando is a good player on the Tangerine Middle School team. He is also suspended several times for his actions during the school year.

Mrs. Hoffman

Mrs. Hoffman is Paul's science teacher at Lake Windsor Middle School.

Dr. Grace Johnson

Dr. Johnson is the principal at Tangerine Middle School.

Mano

Mano is a fullback on the Tangerine Middle School soccer team.

Mars

See Paul Fisher

Mr. Murrow

Mr. Murrow is the head of guidance at Lake Windsor Middle School. His wife is a teacher at Tangerine Middle School.

Mrs. Murrow

Mrs. Murrow is Paul's language arts teacher at Tangerine Middle School. She is the wife of Mr. Murrow, and this fact causes Paul to worry that information about his disability will make its way to Tangerine.

Nita

Nita is the cousin of Maya Pandhi; she is a good player on the Tangerine Middle School soccer team.

Maya Pandhi

Maya is one of the star players for Tangerine Middle School soccer team. She learned to play the sport in England and is featured in Bill Donnelly's article on the star girls on the Tangerine team. Maya is Nita's cousin.

Mrs. Potter

Mrs. Potter is the science teacher at Tangerine Middle School.

Sergeant Rojas

A member of the Tangerine County's Sheriff Department, Sergeant Rojas arrests Arthur for the murder of Luis Cruz. Rojas is in charge of the investigation into the murder.

Antoine Thomas

Antoine Thomas is a senior, the star quarterback of Lake Windsor High School, and the elder brother of Shandra Thomas. By the end of the novel, it is revealed that Antoine has been lying about his residency with the knowledge and help of unnamed others so that he could play football for Lake Windsor. Antoine tells the truth about the matter at the end of the football season, resulting in a nullification of all of Lake Windsor's wins and team records. Antoine proves himself to be a man of honor in another way, as he defends Luis after Arthur hits him, and vows revenge on Erik and Arthur for their actions. Antoine does not like Erik and speaks out against him.

Shandra Thomas

Shandra Thomas is the talented starting goalie on the Tangerine Middle School team. She is the younger sister of Antoine Thomas. Because of that connection and because of Antoine's attendance of Lake Windsor High School, she hides from Bill Donnelly when he comes to write a story about the girls on the Tangerine team.

Tina Turreton

Tina is a student and cheerleader at Lake Windsor High School. She dates Arthur the football player.

Mr. Walski

An eighth-grade teacher at Lake Windsor Middle School, Mr. Walski is also the school's soccer coach. He kicks Paul off the team for insurance reasons when he learns that Paul's file contains the form about his disability. Coach Walski tries to use Paul's alleged ineligibility against the Tangerine Middle School team when they play Lake Windsor at the end of the soccer season.

Mr. Ward

Mr. Ward is Paul's math teacher at Lake Windsor Middle School.

Coach Warner

Coach Warner is the head football coach at Lake Windsor High School. Paul jumps on him at the football awards banquet near the end of the novel to help Tino get free. As a result, Paul is expelled from the school district for the year.

Themes

Truth versus Lies

One of the primary themes in *Tangerine* is the importance of telling the truth and living the truth as well as the consequences of lies. As star football player Antoine Thomas advises Paul toward the end of the novel, "Don't spend your life hiding under the bleachers, little brother. The truth shall set you free." Paul responds, "Yes! Yes!" Truths and falsehoods are important to nearly every plot in *Tangerine*, even secondary ones. Old Charley Burns, for example, takes bribes and does not find out the truth about the poor quality of most of the construction projects in the area. Because of Burns, a sinkhole develops that engulfs the junior high school portable classrooms. As a result, he must resign.

For Paul, the truth about what happened to make him legally blind is very important. He does not remember until the end of the novel that his older brother Erik held him down and convinced his friend Vincent Castor to force spray paint into five-year-old Paul's eyes. Paul's parents have not told the truth to him about what happened to him and allowed Erik's lie about Paul staring at a solar eclipse to become the accepted truth. Such lies have eaten away at the family's interpersonal relationships and perhaps allowed Paul's parents to rationalize not dealing with Erik's problems. Mr. and Mrs. Fisher have let the truth become unimportant in their lives—to their own detriment.

Paul gradually remembers more and more about his personal truth as he observes or helps uncover other characters' truths. For example, Paul can see that Erik and Arthur are destructive and only care about their own personal gain, because the truth does not matter to them. Although Paul does not know that they robbed houses in the neighborhood until his mother reveals that painful truth in a meeting at the Fisher home, he knows other truths about them. For example, Paul witnesses how Erik and Arthur make fun of Mike Costello's death and Joey's immediate reaction to it in front of him and Joey yet Erik and Arthur act respectfully in front of Erik and Paul's mother. Erik puts on a similar front whenever adults are around, but reveals his true mean-spirited nature when alone with his peers or those younger than him.

Topics for Further Study

- Using the Internet, research one of the environmental topics touched on in *Tangerine*, such as muck fires, sinkholes, lightning strikes, or weather extremes in Florida. Create a presentation for the class in which you explain the phenomenon in terms of the novel. Include information about how the topic you choose is relevant to your local environment, if applicable.

- After Paul and his friend try to save the Cruzes's trees, they escape the cold by going into a Quonset hut. Research the history of Quonset huts and how they are used today at your library and on the Internet. Write a research paper that includes your findings and how the huts play a role in the novel.

- In a small group, discuss what you think motivates Erik Fisher to act the way he does. Before you meet with the group, have each member find some information on the psychology or sociology of troubled teens that supports his or her perspective. How do you feel about the "Erik Fisher Football Dream," as Paul calls it, and the breaks often given to sports stars in schools? Present your findings in a short presentation and/or debate for the class.

- At the beginning of *Tangerine*, there is a quotation from a song by the 1960s rock band The Doors called "The Soft Parade." It says, "Successful hills are here to stay. Everything must be this way." In an essay, explain how the song relates to the novel. How do you interpret the quotation, and, perhaps, the song as a whole?

- Watch the film *Bend It Like Beckham* (2002), about a Sikh girl living in England who is obsessed with playing soccer despite her parents' objections. In a paper, compare and contrast the lives and motivations of Jesminder and Paul. How do cultural differences play a role in your interpretation of both the book and the film?

Antoine is one peer who does not respect Erik because he, like Paul, knows that Erik does not respect or care about the truth. Like Paul, Antoine witnesses Erik order Arthur to use a blackjack on Luis Cruz when he confronts Erik and Arthur about hitting his younger brother, Tino, at the Fisher house. This act eventually causes Luis's death, but not before Antoine and a few other football players vow to help Luis get back at Erik and Arthur. One way Antoine hurts Erik is by telling the truth about his eligibility to play at Lake Windsor to Bill Donnelly. Antoine lives in Tangerine, not Lake Windsor, and plays football at Lake Windsor High School with the full knowledge of the staff. By telling the truth, all of Lake Windsor's wins are nullified, as are the school records set during his playing days. This action makes Erik's short-lived career there also essentially off the books. While the adults lie about not knowing where Antoine lived, Antoine is freed by the truth. So is his sister Shandra, who attends Tangerine Middle School and has to hide from Donnelly when he comes to write about the best girl soccer players at the school.

Life and Death

There are three deaths in *Tangerine*—those of Mike Costello, Luis Cruz, and Old Charley Burns—and each one underscores the importance of life and death to the story. Bloor emphasizes the fragility of life and how close people are to death every day, while also using each death as an example of why the truth is important. Mike Costello dies because he was standing next to a goalpost that was struck by lightning. Because of his death, Caroline Fisher works to get football practices moved to a time when lightning strikes are less common. His death also allows Bloor to show how poorly Erik and Arthur behave. Old Charley Burns's death has a similar purpose. He has a heart attack in his lawyer's office after admitting to taking bribes for years and not investigating construction permits. His actions defrauded the people of Tangerine County and contributed to his death. While Mike's death is a tragic accident and Burns's death a tragic result of his own actions, Luis Cruz's death is the most unnecessary of all. Luis plays a key part in his father's life as well as that of his younger siblings. He helps out with the family business, has developed a new type of tangerine that could put the business on the map, and helps out by driving the twins to and from school. Luis also provides a role model for Paul, who can relate to Luis's passion for tangerines and his open nature. Luis ends up dead because he dared to confront Erik and Arthur over their treatment of Tino at Paul's house. Through his confrontation, Luis ends up showing the depth of Erik and Arthur's disrespect of others. Luis's death is the one that compels Paul to fully confront what happened to him and understand the importance of telling the truth. These deaths each bring the truth about many aspects of the story closer to the light.

Favoritism for Sports Stars

Another idea explored in *Tangerine* is the favoritism shown for people who play sports. Paul repeatedly refers to his father's obsession with Erik as a star football player as the "Erik Fisher Football Dream." Mr. Fisher focuses to the exclusion of other things on getting Erik noticed as an extremely talented placekicker. He believes that Erik can play football for a prestigious university, then perhaps professionally, and does whatever he can to help him reach that goal. Mr. Fisher favors Erik to the extreme because of his talent and ignores Paul and his own solid soccer skills. Mr. Fisher insists on attending every one of Erik's football events but never once attends a game of Paul's and knows nothing about what his younger son does as a member of the soccer team. Mrs. Fisher only attends one game of Paul's, the last one played at Lake Windsor Middle School. She does not place as much importance on Erik's star status and does little more than drive him to and from practices and games. Bloor draws a portrait of the parents as favoring Erik, the arrogant high school sports star, over Paul, the handicapped middle school soccer player. This situation allows Paul to have empathy for others and become more certain that the truth is one of the most important things in life. Such favoritism essentially ends when it is revealed that Erik helped rob neighborhood homes and contributed to the death of Luis. However, the mistakes of the parents only serve to build the character of Paul.

Diary-Form Novel

Tangerine is not written as a straight narrative but takes the form of a diary written by Paul Fisher. In place of chapters or other kinds of sections, there are diary entries in which Paul describes the events as he experiences them or understands them. By using such a form, Paul is writing in the first person and everything is filtered through his perspective. Writing in a diary format also allows the character of Paul to express himself in a very personal manner, as a diary is often where people write their innermost thoughts and feelings.

Flashbacks

Scattered throughout *Tangerine* are flashbacks to Paul's past. A *flashback* presents events that occurred before a story began. In Paul's flashbacks, he remembers bits and pieces of the events surrounding the moment when he became legally blind. At the beginning of the novel, Paul reluctantly believes that he was blinded when he looked directly at the sun during an eclipse. His flashbacks are pieces of his memory. Through them, Paul learns that the story about the eclipse is not true and that Erik and his cohort Vincent Castor forced spray paint into Paul's eyes when he was a small child. The flashbacks help Paul understand the power of the truth.

Setting

The setting is important to fully understanding the themes, characters, and plot of *Tangerine*. The *setting* is the time, place, and culture in which the narrative's action takes place. In *Tangerine*, the setting is Lake Windsor, Florida. As newcomers to the area, Paul and his family encounter unexpected extremes in weather (hot and freezing cold), afternoon thunderstorms with lightning, muck fires, and the citrus industry—both active and buried below ground. The novel takes place in a time contemporary to its publication date—1997—but it is the place and culture of this part of Florida that Bloor uses as a backdrop to the novel's situations and dilemmas. Some aspects of the setting in the novel include the many residential developments, the racial makeup of the characters, and an emphasis on football culture.

Symbolism

Bloor uses some aspects of the setting of *Tangerine* in a symbolic fashion. In fiction, *symbols* are something that suggests something else without losing their original meaning. In *Tangerine*, Bloor uses symbols that have meaning from their function in the story. For example, the muck fires that continuously blaze and cannot be put out can be seen as a symbol of the long-running fire in the Fisher family over Erik's role in the blinding of Paul and in other transgressions. The sinkhole at the middle school and the termite infestation in parts of Paul's neighborhood also can be interpreted as having symbolic value. The sinkhole symbolizes the greed of such men as Old Charley Burns as well as the emptiness of Lake Windsor, while the termite infestation symbolizes the problematic foundation on which Lake Windsor society is based.

Florida

Because of its warm and sunny climate, Florida has seen many cycles of economic growth since it became a state in 1845. It was not until the early twentieth century that Florida became a major tourist center and saw its population greatly increase. After World War II, Florida's population grew because the state became a favorite place for millions of Americans from the North to spend their retirement years. In the late twentieth century, Florida again experienced a booming population and became one of the fastest-growing states in the country.

By 1990, Florida was the fourth-largest state in terms of population, with nearly thirteen million residents, yet only about thirty percent of Florida's residents had been born in that state. Ten years later, Florida was the third-most populated state with nearly sixteen million residents. Aside from retirees, many American newcomers (often from the Northeast and the Midwest) came to take advantage of growing new business enterprises such as the high-tech, banking, and service industries often tied to U.S. Department of Defense contracts and the vast presence of many U.S. military facilities in the state. Florida also saw its population increase because of large-scale migration from countries in the Caribbean and Latin America, especially Cuba and Haiti.

The rapid population growth created issues for Florida in the 1990s. As the average age of the newcomer population lowered in the 1980s and 1990s, there was a greater demand for schools. By the 1990s, schools in Florida had become overcrowded because of the increased number of students. This situation contributed to the use of portable classrooms for whole grades at Lake Windsor Middle School in *Tangerine*. This growing population also put a strain on Florida's natural environment, as resources such as timber and minerals became increasingly exploited. To safeguard the remaining natural environment, the state of Florida created the Department of Environmental Protection in 1993 to implement pollution control laws, better manage water resources, protect coastal and marine resources, and purchase environmentally endangered land tracts.

Citrus Industry

The citrus industry had been part of Florida's history since the late sixteenth century, when citrus trees and shrubs were introduced by the Spanish to the area (as well as to California). By the time Florida became a state in 1845, big groves of wild citrus trees could be found in many forests. The process of domestication soon began, and small groves were planted in the 1830s, although lack of transportation meant that citrus agriculture could not be commercialized until railways reached the interior of the state in the 1870s and 1880s. At that time groves became larger, as crops were able to be shipped and sold out of state. Despite several major freezes in the late nineteenth and early twentieth centuries that destroyed many citrus trees, Florida growers continued to revive the industry, which rapidly expanded throughout the twentieth century. The state became the dominant producer of citrus in the United States by the 1960s. By the early 2000s, Florida produced the vast majority of America's oranges and grapefruits. Florida was also the largest producer of tangerines, which had been introduced to the state in 1876. By 2000, the tangerine industry in Florida brought in $60 million per year. Although Florida's economy has become more diversified over the years, citrus agriculture remained one of the state's leading industries in the 1990s and continued to be into the twenty-first century.

Critical Overview

Tangerine was widely praised from the time it was published in 1997. Critics and readers alike embraced the book for the way Bloor draws his characters, develops the plot, and depicts life in Florida. Commenting on the audio-book version of the novel, Bette D. Ammon of *Kliatt* called *Tangerine* a "strange and riveting story" and "first-rate." In the *Massachusetts Sunday Telegram*, Nicholas A. Basbanes writes that Bloor "has written a powerful novel that is rich in regional nuance and purpose." Basbanes concludes by labeling the novel "an impressive debut."

Some critics found fault with a few aspects of the novel, although not with the novel as a whole. While Kathleen Squires in *Booklist* believes that the development of Bloor's characters outside of Paul is thin and the story a bit busy, she praises the book overall, calling it a "dark debut novel," and she lauds the "atmospheric portrait of an eerie community." *Publishers Weekly* takes issue with the way Bloor leaves some elements unresolved and with his pacing, but praises him, too: "first-novelist Bloor pulls it off, wedding athletic heroics to American gothic with a fluid touch and a flair for dialogue." The review concludes that *Tangerine* is "A sports novel that breaks the mold."

While some reviewers focused on the sports element of the story, other critics praised its environmental aspects. In the *School Library Journal*, Linda K. Ferguson and Joy Sibley write that *Tangerine* "is an excellent example of the conflict between humans and nature." Ferguson and Sibley conclude, "Aside from the conflicts between humans and nature (they just keep coming), the story is filled with humorous yet poignant middle school scenes."

Young readers were also impressed. One young reviewer in the *Hamilton Spectator* comments, "I thought it was really good. It really paints a clear picture in your mind of what's going on. It's a little fuzzy sometimes about what's happening, but it's still good."

What Do I Read Next?

- *Story Time*, published in 2004, is a young adult novel by Edward Bloor. This humorous ghost story focuses on issues of testing and charter schools through the adventures of young teen protagonists.

- *Who Really Killed Cock Robin?*, published in 1985, is a young adult novel by Jean George, which features some friends who follow the life of a bird and eventually investigate why it dies.

- *Crusader*, published in 1999, is the second young adult novel by Bloor. The novel focuses on fifteen-year-old Roberta Ritter, who lives in south Florida and works at a virtual-reality arcade at a failing mall. She struggles with the lack of positive role models and the racist games played at the arcade while hoping for a career as a journalist.

- *London Calling*, published in 2005, is a young adult novel by Bloor. In the novel, Martin Conway, an eighth-grade misfit attending a prep school in New Jersey, inherits an old radio that allows him to travel back in time to London in the 1940s.

- *Touchdown Pass*, originally published in 1948, is a young adult novel by Clair Bee. This is the first in a long series of sports novels featuring Chip Hilton that Bloor said he read when he was a child and that they influenced his desire to write.

Chip is already a football star in high school when he helps discover who committed an act of sabotage.

- *The Absolutely True Diary of a Part-Time Indian*, published in 2007, is a young adult novel by Sherman Alexie. The novel explores issues of identity as a young Native American teenager, Arnold Spirit, transfers from the reservation school to a rich white school. He must deal with issues of identity and fitting in while also confronting problems in his personal life.

- *Go for the Goal: A Champion's Guide to Winning in Soccer and Life*, published in 1999, is a nonfiction book by Mia Hamm and Aaron Heifetz. This book written by Hamm, a soccer champion, and her coauthor includes biographical and instructional information, as well as words to inspire the reader.

Sources

Ammon, Bette D., Review of *Tangerine*, in *Kliatt*, Vol. 36, No. 2, March 2002, p. 53.

Basbanes, Nicholas A., "This spring's offerings seem to run the gamut," in *Sunday Telegram*, April 6, 1997, p. C5.

Bloor, Edward, *Tangerine*, Harcourt Brace & Company, 1997.

Broderick-Price, Brian, "*Tangerine* Offers Action," in *Hamilton Spectator*, September 2, 2000, p. K03.

Comerford, Lynda Brill, "Flying Starts: Children's Authors and Artists Talk About Their Spring '97 Debuts," in *Publishers Weekly*, Vol. 244, No. 26, June 30, 1997, p. 26.

Ferguson, Linda K., and Joy Sibley, "Middle Schoolers Take on the Issues," in *School Library Journal*, June 1999, pp. 34-35.

Flowers, Sarah, Review of *Tangerine*, in *School Library Journal*, March 2002, p. 87.

Review of *Tangerine*, in *Publishers Weekly*, Vol. 244, No. 12, March 24, 1997, p. 84.

Squires, Kathleen, Review of *Tangerine*, in *Booklist*, Vol. 93, No. 18, May 15, 1997, p. 1573.

Further Reading

Alexander, Sally Hobart, *Taking Hold: My Journey into Blindness*, Simon & Schuster Children's Publishing, 1994.

> This young adult memoir tells the story of a teacher in her twenties who suddenly goes blind and how she deals with the changes in her life.

Friend, Sandra, *Sinkholes*, Pineapple Press, 2002.

> This young adult book explains why sinkholes occur and illustrates the text with pictures of sinkholes from around the world.

Laszlo, Pierre, *Citrus: A History*, University of Chicago Press, 2007.

> This book provides a history of citrus worldwide, from its roots in Southeast Asia to Africa and Europe, and finally to the Americas in the 1500s. Laszlo also explores how citrus affected various aspects of life, culture, religion, agriculture, and the arts.

Mormino, Gary R., *Land of Sunshine, State of Dreams: A Social History of Modern Florida*, University Press of Florida, 2008.

> This social history of Florida

chronicles its cycles of development from its days as a Spanish colony to its phenomenal growth at the end of the twentieth century and the beginning of the twenty-first century.

CPSIA information can be obtained
at www.ICGtesting.com
Printed in the USA
LVOW03s2206010118

561466LV00039B/1103/P